TAKING ACTION ON CLIMATE CHANGE

BURNING UP
Escalating Heat Waves and Forest Fires

ALEX DAVID

Cavendish Square

New York

Published in 2020 by Cavendish Square Publishing, LLC
243 5th Avenue, Suite 136, New York, NY 10016
Copyright © 2020 by Cavendish Square Publishing, LLC

First Edition

Website: cavendishsq.com

Library of Congress Cataloging-in-Publication Data

Names: David, Alex, author.
Title: Burning up : escalating heat waves and forest fires / Alex David.
Description: New York : Cavendish Square, 2020. | Series: Taking action on climate change |
Includes bibliographical references and index. | Audience: Grade 5 to 8.
Identifiers: LCCN 2019010035 (print) | LCCN 2019016177 (ebook) |
ISBN 9781502652249 (ebook) | ISBN 9781502652232 (library bound) |
ISBN 9781502652225 (pbk.)
Subjects: LCSH: Heat waves (Meteorology)--Juvenile literature. |
Forest fires--Juvenile literature. | Climatic changes--Juvenile literature.
Classification: LCC QC981.8.A5 (ebook) | LCC QC981.8.A5 D38 2020 (print) |
DDC 551.5/253--dc23
LC record available at https://lccn.loc.gov/2019010035

Copy Editor: Nathan Heidelberger
Associate Art Director: Alan Sliwinski
Designer: Ginny Kemmerer
Production Coordinator: Karol Szymczuk
Photo Research: J8 Media

The photographs in this book are used by permission and through the courtesy of:
Cover, Colin Dewar/Shutterstock.com; p. 4 Gamblin Yann/Paris Match Archive/Getty Images;
p. 8 DNetromphotos/Shutterstock.com; p. 12 Brett Deering/Getty Images;
p. 14 trgrowth/Shutterstock.com; p. 16 plherrera/E+/Getty Images; p. 17 Glen Fergus,
own work/File: Global monthly temperature record.png/Wikimedia Commons/CCA 3.0
Unported; p. 20 Earl D. Walker/Shutterstock.com; p. 22 Carla Gottgens/Bloomberg/
Getty Images; p. 24 Saeed Khan/AFP/Getty Images; p. 25 Bo Rader/Wichita
Eagle/TNS/Getty Images; p. 28 Efured/Shutterstock.com; p. 29 Seigfred Geil
Gregory Caete/EyeEm/Getty Images; p. 30 Justin Sullivan/Getty Images;
p. 32 JEAN-FRANCOIS MONIER/AFP/Getty Images; p. 34 KEN CEDENO/UPI/Newscom;
p. 36 JUNG YEON-JE/AFP/Getty Images; p. 38 Predrag Vuckovic/E+/Getty Images;
p. 39 Billy Hustace/The Image Bank/Getty Images; p. 42 Karl Mondon/Digital First Media/
The Mercury News/Getty Images; p. 50 Daniel Bockwoldt/picture alliance/Getty Images.

Printed in the United States of America

Portions of this book originally appeared in *Adapting to Severe Heat Waves* by Tamra B. Orr.

CONTENTS

Julia Butterfly Hill triumphantly stands on her tree, Luna.

Introduction

Julia Butterfly Hill could feel the rough bark of her tree, "Luna," on her bare feet. High above the ground—180 feet (55 meters)—Hill was alone in the tree. However, it was not just any tree—it was a very symbolic tree: a gigantic redwood she was trying to save from being cut down. She spent 738 days in Luna and was able to convince the lumber company to spare not just Luna from their chainsaws but also the trees that covered the 200 feet (61 m) surrounding Luna.

Hill is just one example of an environmental activist who is trying to change the way we treat our planet. Activists and scientists are doing important work.

The Anthropocene

The history of our planet is defined by ages. You've probably heard of the Jurassic period. This was millions of years ago. Now, we are in a different age. There is even a professional organization that decides the current name of the age. It is called the International Union of Geological Sciences (IUGS). It has labeled our age the Holocene age. It is named this because of the type of rock deposits that are on Earth's surface now. However, experts in climate science want the current age to have a different name, the Anthropocene.

Anthropocene means "the age of humans." This new classification indicates that we are living in a time when our ideas of nature are being completely reexamined. Instead of nature being something that is separate from humans, we are realizing that human beings are actively changing nature—and not in a good way.

Human interference with nature was minimal before the Industrial Revolution, but ever since the nineteenth century, when humans started mass-producing goods and creating large-scale carbon emissions, Earth's ecosystem has quickly changed. You probably have heard news stories about forest fires in California, or maybe you have experienced very hot temperatures firsthand. Climate change has caused both of these events.

Climate change is caused by the heating of the planet, which is also known as global warming. Earth's temperature has risen about 1.8 degrees Fahrenheit

(1 degree Celsius) since before the Industrial Revolution. This is happening because humans are burning lots of fossil fuels, like coal, oil, and gas. This creates the greenhouse effect. Greenhouse gases accumulate in Earth's atmosphere and trap heat. Therefore, the planet warms up. This extra heat is causing all kinds of damage. The ice caps are melting, countries are experiencing droughts, animals are becoming endangered, and people are running out of food. It is not a good situation.

Informed Change

So, what should we do? Sit around and worry? Watch from the sidelines and hope it stops? Pretend that it is normal? The best thing to do is to be informed, to change our lifestyles, and to try to encourage policy change. In 2015, countries from all over the world met at the UN's climate change conference in Paris to discuss what each country could do. They decided to slow the heating down as much as possible, setting a goal of no more than 3.6°F (2°C). We don't want Earth to heat up any more, so if we can change the way we live, invest in new technologies, and work together, life might have a chance of surviving. Heat waves and forest fires are two disastrous effects of global warming, but people are realizing what must be done. Young people, especially, are participating in a climate change revolution. They are refusing to be quiet, and just like Julia Butterfly Hill, they are saving the planet.

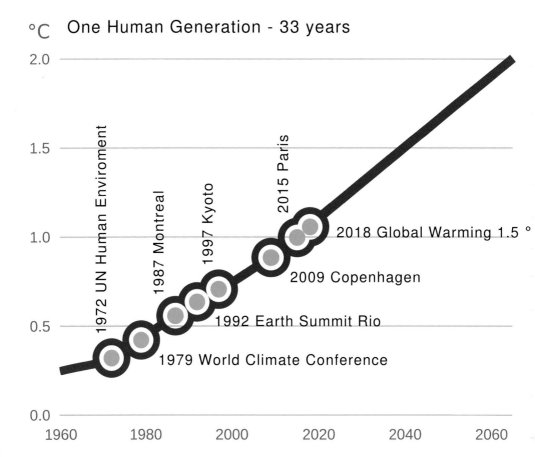

°C One Human Generation - 33 years

2.0

1.5

1972 UN Human Enviroment

1987 Montreal

1997 Kyoto

2015 Paris

1.0   2018 Global Warming 1.5 °

2009 Copenhagen

1992 Earth Summit Rio

0.5

1979 World Climate Conference

0.0

1960   1980   2000   2020   2040   2060

This graph shows Earth's rising temperatures,
along with dates and locations of major
environmental meetings. In 2018, a report was
released about what would happen if Earth's
temperature rose by 1.5 degrees Celsius.

CHAPTER 1

It's Getting Hot in Here

Some people would say there's no better season than summer. The heat and the sun lead to happiness and good times. The truth is, many places in the United States experience the warm dog days of summer, but sometimes the temperature goes up too much and things become not just uncomfortable but also dangerous. This happens not just in the United States but also around the world.

The Difference Between Hot and Too Hot

According to climate scientist Monika Barcikowska, since the 1900s, the temperature has risen about 1.8°F (1°C). If the average temperature rises by another half degree, it may double the amount of people exposed to extreme heat. In the summer of 2018 in Pakistan and Iran, temperatures were above 129°F (54°C). As the temperatures rose over a three-day period, sixty-five people were killed. This is not just a typical summer but something else. It's a heat wave, and it's dangerous.

What's the difference between temperatures that let you enjoy lemonade on the beach and heat so intense you can't go outside because you might end up in the hospital from heatstroke?

The difference between typical summer weather and a heat wave is simple. First, the temperature goes up more than expected. Second, the humidity—the amount of moisture in the air—is often higher than usual. Higher humidity makes high temperatures feel even hotter. Third, higher-than-normal temperatures and humidity last longer than is typical.

What causes high temperatures, high humidity, and the prolonged presence of both to coincide? At first, a system of high atmospheric pressure moves into an area. This pulls air from the upper levels of the atmosphere toward the ground. When this happens, the air gets hotter. It also makes it very difficult for other weather systems to come in and push the hot air away, which is one reason heat waves linger for so long. The longer the system stays in one area, the hotter the temperatures are likely to grow. No refreshing breezes can get in when these systems are in place.

The problem is further compounded when stagnant air combines with pollutants such as smog, dust, ozone, and exhaust from vehicles and factories. When the already stagnant air typical of heat waves combines with pollutants that aren't being dispersed by wind or rain, a toxic air haze settles over a city, making it hard to breathe and very dangerous for those with respiratory diseases or compromised immune systems.

Regions in the United States at Risk

What makes one area more vulnerable to heat waves than another? There are a number of factors. One of the first is how hot a normal summer might be in a particular region. Areas like Texas and Arizona are more at risk, for example, than Montana or Colorado. On the other hand, even though heat waves may be more common in typically hotter areas, they are not necessarily as dangerous. Why? The people who live where it gets hot regularly are prepared for it. They already have air conditioning in their houses and cars. They own cool clothes and know how to avoid the hottest parts of the day. People in areas where hot weather is less common do not always have these protections in place, so they end up being far more vulnerable when triple digits arrive. They are not used to dealing with intense heat and have not had the chance to acclimatize.

Heat Waves Heating Up

Heat waves are nothing new. They have been happening on the planet for as long as it has existed. High temperatures have shown up in multiple weather records since they were first kept. Why are scientists so concerned about these temperature changes now?

The main reason for the growing worry is that these heat waves are increasing in intensity and frequency. Enough research has been conducted, compiled, and analyzed to definitively reveal that heat waves are occurring more often and that, as time passes, the temperatures are slowly going up, degree by degree. An occasional heat wave is uncomfortable. For some people, it is extraordinarily dangerous. If heat waves were rare, they would not be a major concern, but this is not the case.

In July of 2011, Oklahoma City, Oklahoma, had twenty-eight days of 100°F (38°C) weather.

Nearly every scientific study supports the near certainty that heat waves are going to be an increasing part of the world's future climate.

A 2010 study from Stanford University stated that there was no doubt that the tropics and parts of the Northern Hemisphere would experience an irreversible rise in summer temperatures within twenty to sixty years. It also stated that by the year 2070, these increases would be largely felt in China, Europe, and throughout most of North America. "Using a large suite of climate model experiments, we see a clear emergence of much more intense, hot conditions in the US within the next three decades," states Professor Noah Diffenbaugh, lead author of the Stanford study. "In the next 30 years, we could see an increase in heat waves like the kind that swept across Europe in 2003 that caused tens of thousands of fatalities."

Trapped Heat

Why are heat waves occurring more often, and why are predictions for the future so dire? Although there is some debate over the answers to these questions, the majority of experts believe it is due to the complications arising from global warming.

The cause of this temperature increase, according to research, is the greenhouse effect. If you have ever walked inside a greenhouse, you might know just how this works. It is always warm inside a greenhouse because the glass lets the heat of the sun in and traps it there. Earth is surrounded by a layer

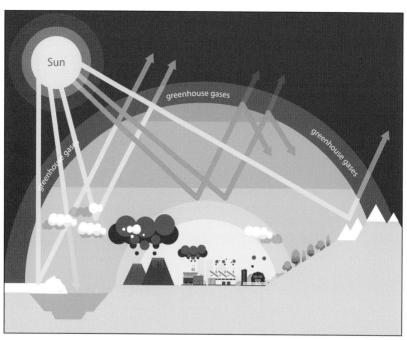

This is an illustration of the greenhouse effect.

of atmosphere that works almost like that greenhouse glass. It lets some of the sun's heat through to the planet to keep it warm, and the ground absorbs the heat. The rest bounces off of Earth's surface back into space. When this outgoing reflected heat meets greenhouse gases in the atmosphere, however, it becomes trapped there. As a result, temperatures of the air and water below rise, and the planet gets warmer.

For more than two centuries, humans have emitted heat-trapping gases like carbon dioxide, nitrous oxide, methane, and halocarbons into the atmosphere. These are by-products of our modern world and the machines that run it, from factory

THE DIFFERENCE BETWEEN CLIMATE AND WEATHER

During the middle of a blizzard, people may ask themselves, "If global warming is happening, why is it so cold out?" The answer lies in the difference between climate and weather. "Climate" refers to how the atmosphere changes over a longer span of time, whereas "weather" refers to a short period of shifting temperatures. Therefore, it can be very cold in winter, but climate change is still happening because of global warming. In fact, colder winters might be a sign of climate change.

smokestacks to car tailpipes. Think of all the things humans use that require the burning of oil and gas—cars, buses, ovens, and factories that make all of the products we use every day. Can you imagine a world where we didn't rely on these items? What if everyone used bikes instead of driving cars? What if we didn't produce more stuff but refurbished and tailored the items we already had? Think of all the ideas we could come up with for changing the greenhouse effect. Lifestyle changes like these are needed to change the planet.

Smog is created from cars during rush hour. This is a visible sign of air pollution and the greenhouse effect.

One of the most prevalent greenhouse gases in the atmosphere is carbon dioxide. It is produced all over the planet by the burning of fossil fuels—coal, oil, and natural gas. Another gas is methane, which is twenty times more effective at trapping heat than carbon dioxide. It comes from a number of sources—some natural, such as volcanoes, animal by-products, and the melting of the permafrost, and some man-made, such as large landfills, natural gas systems, coal mining, and chemical fertilizers. As these two gases, carbon dioxide and methane, increase in the atmosphere, so, too, do the harmful effects of global warming.

Has global warming ever occurred before? Gradual warming and cooling have occurred many times over the history of this planet in cycles of natural variation. However, the key word here is "gradual." What is happening now, thanks to the modern, industrialized lifestyles of humans, is not gradual. It is happening faster than at any other time in the history of the world, and scientists are worried.

Too Hot to Hold

Heat waves can severely damage urban infrastructure. High temperatures can cause concrete and other building and paving materials to buckle and collapse. Freeways can become unusable and bridges unreliable if they remain too hot for long periods of time. In 2018, a Chicago bridge became so hot that it could no work properly. The surface temperature of the steel bridge reached 100°F (38°C). The joints swelled in the heat, and it could not open for boats that needed to pass through underneath.

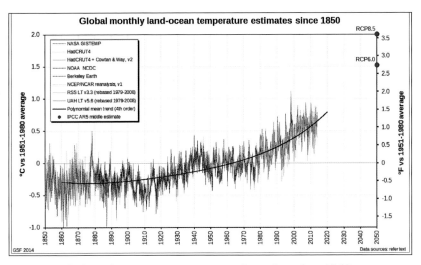

This graph shows how average temperatures have risen since 1850.

WHAT'S HALF A DEGREE?

The Paris Agreement hopes to prevent temperatures from rising by 2°C (3.6°F). Ideally, it hopes to limit the increase to only 1.5°C (2.7°F) above pre-industrial levels. That does not seem like much, but experts at the European Geosciences Union discovered that if Earth's temperature rises that half a degree celsius (0.9°F) more, there will be serious consequences. Heat waves will last one-third longer. Tropical coral reefs, which would be able to survive at 1.5°C (2.7°F), will die at 2°C (3.6°F). Crops like corn and soy will suffer at 2°C (3.6°F) because high temperatures will prevent critical parts of development and may make pathogens and pests more likely to attack the vulnerable crops. Therefore, what seems like a small increase actually has profound consequences.

The fire department had to come and spray water on the bridge so that it could cool off.

It's not just steel bridges that are in danger during a heat wave, but many other types of urban infrastructure as well. Buildings, sidewalks, and roads made out of asphalt or concrete can reach 140°F (60°C) during a heat crisis.

One of the most pressing concerns with heat waves is their potential threat to nuclear power plants. Many of these plants rely on lake or river water for cooling purposes. When heat waves warm that water, the cooling effect is lessened, increasing the chance of nuclear accidents. Many plants have to cut back drastically on their production during heat waves, just at the moment when more power is needed by overheated utility customers to power their fans and air conditioners.

A rise of a few degrees in average global temperatures may not seem like much. However, as the triple digits arrive—and hang around day after day—the dominoes will begin to fall. Where they will stop and where that will leave us, no one is sure. However, the fact that heat waves will only grow stronger and more frequent is something most of the world's scientists agree on.

Threat to Crops

Heat waves also cause problems with flash flooding because the higher temperatures melt winter snows and ice sheets faster and earlier than is normal. In some regions of the world, this early melting can also result in avalanches. On the other hand, extreme heat in other areas of the world exacerbates (worsens) already serious drought conditions. Warmer ocean temperatures also lead to an increase in the number of hurricanes and can cause the formation of stronger inland thunderstorms and blizzards.

Drought distresses cornstalks in a cornfield.

Higher temperatures are damaging to agriculture as well. "Those kind of severe heat events also put enormous stress on major crops like corn, soybean, cotton, and wine grapes, causing a significant reduction in yields," Noah Diffenbaugh stated in the previously mentioned Stanford climate study. Droughts and flash floods can also destroy a crop quickly.

In California, fruit is highly sensitive to shifts in temperatures. During a July 2018 heat wave, rising temperatures that lasted more than fourteen days made fruit like apricots brown quickly. For example, instead of losing a normal 5 or 10 percent of their crop, some farmers lost 40 percent of their crop yield during the California heat wave. This happened all over the state. From avocados to prunes to Valencia oranges, different farm products suffered from the prolonged heat. Food sources for animals also change during atmospheric shifts, so birds end up eating more of the crops in the field. This shows how heat waves don't just put stress on infrastructure but also on agriculture. This is in addition to the community stress that heat waves cause for people. As we saw in the Pakistan example, people are at risk of death during heat waves.

Predictions for the Future

In Europe, an organization called DRIAS projects that there will be an increase in heat waves. They predict that in 2035 heat waves could occur for five consecutive days at a time. In 2080, they believe heat waves could occur for ten to forty days at a time.

Heat waves are difficult disasters that cause people to stay indoors and to seek emergency relief. They fundamentally stress agriculture and infrastructure, causing changes in food prices and transportation. They also put human-centered ecosystems at risk for forest fires.

FIRE DANGER RATING TODAY

LOW-MODERATE HIGH VERY HIGH SEVERE EXTREME CODE RED

This sign from 2019 warned drivers of fires in Australia.

CHAPTER 2

Heat Waves and Forest Fires

Humans live in ecosystems. These communities include plants and animals that all respond to one another. Heat waves may seem like isolated natural occurrences that make temperatures hot for a few days and then everything goes back to normal, but this is not the case. Heat waves cause many other problems for an ecosystem. By increasing temperatures so dramatically, they suck up the water supply, causing droughts to happen. Droughts, in turn, causes areas of vegetation to dry up. This makes large areas of vegetation susceptible to fire. Alternatively, heat waves also cause flash flooding, as they melt snow. Let's take a closer look at how ecosystems function and how they're affected by these events.

During the 2019 Australian Open tennis tournament, a man finds refuge from the heat in a mist fan.

Ripple Effects

Nature is always working to maintain a balance. Too much or too little of only one element or variable can tip these invisible scales and create many problems. Introducing a new animal into an environment, for example, can create a ripple effect throughout an ecosystem. The new species may start using food sources that other animals need, endangering those animals' survival.

When the average temperature of a region changes, even if it is only by a degree or two, the same ripple effect occurs. Increased heat, for example, means drier forests and much higher risks of forest fires. In 2019, Australia suffered a five-day heat wave. Temperatures reached 120°F (48.8°C). In New South Wales, nine temperature records were broken. Australia was already in the middle of a seven-year drought, but the heat wave put the region at risk for bushfires. In Tasmania, an island off Australia's southern coast, fires destroyed homes. Residents had to flee the area, and national parks were closed. In Western Australia, wildfires also broke out in Perth. Over eighty firefighters had to try to contain the blaze.

Just in the same way that heat waves can make ecosystems drier, they can also make them wetter. Heat waves cause problems with flash flooding because the higher temperatures melt winter snows and ice sheets faster and earlier than normal. In some regions of the world, this early melting can also result in avalanches. In 2014, a heat wave raised the temperature in Alaska by 40°F (22°C). This created numerous ripple effects. Ski resorts closed down, and the 2014 Yukon Quest sled dog race had to change the location of its finish line so that fans of the race wouldn't fall through the ice of a melting river.

The warm temperatures were not actually due to weather patterns on the land, but rather in the Pacific Ocean. A

A wildfire in Kansas burns a grain elevator in 2017.

MEGAFIRES

It's not just forests that are at risk to burn. Prairies, like those on the Great Plains, can also react to hot and dry conditions. On March 6, 2017, the Northwest Complex Fire burned parts of Oklahoma, Texas, and Kansas. In Oklahoma alone, it swept through 781,000 acres (316,060 hectares). In Texas, it burned 482,000 acres (195,060 ha). All told, about 2 million acres (809,370 ha) of land were affected. This fire is classified as a megafire since it burned more than 100,000 acres (40,470 ha).

high-pressure ridge took rain and warm air that California usually received up to Alaska. This weather system made January of 2014 one of the warmest winters for the region. A balmy 62°F (16.7°C) was recorded on January 27.

The Relationship Between Heat Waves and Forest Fires

Forest fires occur when there are heat waves because heat waves cause droughts and sometimes remove humidity from the soil and the air. This means that any vegetation quickly turns from being green and fire resistant to dry tinder, perfect for a fire.

Forest fires pose a risk to people who live in areas of densely populated forests and ecosystems that experience drought. In the United States, California has experienced many forest fires because of the lack of water in its ecosystem. The vegetation becomes extremely dry. When extreme temperatures occur, vegetation is likely to combust or to catch fire from fires that were not properly put out or from sparking electrical lines. High temperatures also dry out water sources that could be used to stop the fire, like lakes and rivers.

Humans Hurt and Humans Help

Although sometimes fires happen because of lightning or combustion, many times they happen as a result of a leftover campfire, barbecue coals, or people throwing cigarette butts into foliage. When the vegetation is highly flammable, it does not take much to start a fire. The fire can spread quickly, making it difficult for firefighters to react in time.

Once a fire starts, it is often difficult to put out. Wind conditions cause forest fires to move in unpredictable ways. Forest roads are often very narrow, making it hard for firefighters' trucks to get through. The effects of climate change can further complicate matters. For instance, in the 2015 California wildfires, fire teams worried they would not have enough water to put out the fire. Their normal water sources had dried out due to the previous drought. Firefighters had to travel longer distances to find sources of water.

THIRSTY YET?

Water is needed to decrease your chance of dehydration.

Dehydration is one of the most dangerous but also most easily overlooked symptoms of heat stress. It is easy to become unbalanced when you lose more liquid through sweat than you gain by drinking, but it is also hard to detect when you have lost that critical hydration balance. Here is a chart to show you what you might feel if you aren't keeping properly hydrated.

Degree of dehydration	Liquid loss (liters) for a 154-pound (70 kg) person	Symptoms
2%	1.4 (0.4 gallon)	thirst
4%	2.8 (0.7 gallon)	thirst and dry mouth
6%	4.2 (1.1 gallons)	all of the above, plus increased heart rate and body temperature
8%	5.6 (1.5 gallons)	all of the above, plus swollen tongue, difficulty with speech, reduced mental and physical performance
12%	8.4 (2.2 gallons)	all of the above, plus recovery is only possible with intravenous fluid administration
14%	9.8 (2.6 gallons)	all of the above, plus rapid temperature increase and death

Firefighters put out a fire at night.

As mentioned, nature is cyclical, and sometimes part of the ecosystem goes out of balance, causing a small disturbance. Interferences, like insect outbreaks or the occasional fire, are natural to forest ecosystems. However, fires are occurring more and more in response to the high temperatures and droughts that are happening because of climate change. Forests that burn from a fire are not necessarily safe from other fires in the future. Sometimes a fire will burn up all flammable vegetation and leave behind fireproof trees and bushes. This makes a forest less likely to be impacted by later fires. However, sometimes a fire will burn a forest and the forest will regrow. The forest will then have even more timber and foliage that is prime fuel for another forest fire.

In 2017, the conifer forests of North America were hit exceptionally hard. For example, the Tubbs Fire in Sonoma County was the deadliest fire the state of California had ever had. Then, however, came the 2018 forest fires in California. A fire called the Camp Fire killed eighty-eight people, and two hundred people were proclaimed missing. This fire also destroyed fourteen thousand residences. Scientists predict fires will increase in California, so people are realizing that forest fire prevention is essential. The government has created laws that forbid people from leaving open fires. They also advise people to clear forests around their properties. The trees surrounding electrical lines are being cleared, and pathways into forests are being expanded. These are some of the many ways humans are adapting to the continuous threats of climate change.

What to Do in a Forest Fire

Forest fires can happen quickly, leaving people to make quick decisions about what to do. First and foremost, if asked to

In 2018, a home burns in the California Camp Fire.

evacuate your home, make sure to do so. This is the best possible way of avoiding injury or death. Before evacuating, prepare your home for fire prevention. Shut off all natural gas supplies. Shut doors to avoid draft. Put on protective clothing like boots or sneakers that will protect you from ash and burning ground. If you have time, fill large vessels, like bathtubs and sinks, with water to discourage fire from spreading throughout your home.

However, if the fire comes on too quickly for police to evacuate you and your community, take these precautions:

Find a water source, like a pond or river, to crouch in.

If there isn't any water nearby, put water on your clothes and find a clearing where there is little vegetation. Lie low in short grass.

Avoid breathing in smoke by putting a wet cloth up to your face. This will allow you to breathe in air without being at risk of smoke inhalation.

Forest fires are a scary effect of heat waves and droughts. These natural disasters will not go away until we can slow the heating of Earth. We are left wondering what to do. Luckily, humans are finding many creative solutions to address this problem. Instead of thinking of an apocalyptic future, many climate scientists, activists, and ordinary citizens are rallying together to find ways to ensure a better future for generations to come.

Taiko, a polar bear, has an ice cube
to help him cool down.

CHAPTER 3

Creative Solutions

Heat waves call for inventive strategies for keeping humans and animals cool. During one heat wave on the East Coast in 2010, zookeepers at the Franklin Park Zoo in Boston, Massachusetts, gave the lions and tigers special treats—"bloodsicles." These icy cold treats were made from 5 gallons (19 liters) of frozen blood. It was one way to keep the big cats cool!

Heat waves require adaptation, both for animals and humans. In an ideal world, we would have already figured out climate change. We would have found ways to curb the amount of carbon dioxide and methane we put into the atmosphere. Since we haven't, we need to adapt. One example might be switching from mostly gas-powered cars to mostly electricity-powered

In 2018, Representative Kathy Castor holds a press conference as part of the House Energy and Commerce Committee.

cars. While total prevention of heat waves and forest fires is not yet possible, there are conferences, programs, and reports that are designed to mitigate, or lessen, the effect of the heat and help people better respond and adapt to rising temperatures.

Federal Responses to Climate Crisis

In December 2018, Nancy Pelosi selected Representative Kathy Castor to champion a committee in Congress to address the climate crisis. The committee was created to make policy recommendations and highlight the number of dangers that will happen in the future because of climate change. Castor stated that she would urgently try to reduce carbon pollution and create more clean energy jobs.

In November of 2018, the government issued a federal report detailing the dangers that Castor is dealing with. The report is called "The Fourth National Climate Assessment" and includes a comprehensive look at climate change. It asks Americans to consider an adaptation and mitigation approach. It puts a spotlight on aspects of our society that will be most impacted by natural disasters related to climate change, including the economy, water systems, communities, indigenous persons, and ecosystems. Natural disasters will not affect all Americans equally and will make life more difficult for people who are already vulnerable. Economic inequality affects disaster preparedness and response. Impoverished people will have a hard time obtaining limited resources, such as crops and clean water.

Green New Deal

Some members of the government are pushing for the Green New Deal. It is a proposed plan that will ask Americans to switch from nuclear energy and fossil fuels to 100 percent green energy by 2030. The collective writers of the idea state, "Building on the concept of FDR's New Deal, we call for a massive mobilization of our communities, government and the people on the scale of World War II—to transition our energy system and economy to 100% clean, renewable energy by 2030, including a complete phase out of fossil fuels, fracked gas and nuclear power." The deal aims to prevent income inequality by replacing jobs created by the fossil fuel industry with clean energy jobs. The Green New

Deal is concerned with the vulnerable members of our society and hopes to protect low-income communities and people of color. It proposes such solutions as offshore wind, geothermal, tidal, and solar energy.

However, as of 2019 the Green New Deal has not been implemented. It would require the support of the president to become a reality.

Intergovernmental Panel on Climate Change

The Intergovernmental Panel on Climate Change (IPCC) is a collection of scientists and researchers joined together by the United Nations. Its aim is to report findings about global climate change and to make suggestions that would help the entire planet.

In 2018, the IPCC held a conference in Incheon, a city in South Korea.

In 2018, they put together a report on how to reduce carbon emissions so that humans could reverse the effects of global warming. Their goal is to keep temperatures from rising more than 2.7°F (1.5°C) above pre-industrial levels.

Paris Agreement

On December 12, 2015, the Paris Agreement asked participating countries to pledge to reduce their carbon emissions so as to prevent Earth from heating more than 3.6°F (2°C). Like the IPCC, however, the agreement hopes to further limit warming to no more than 2.7°F (1.5°C). As of February 2019, 195 countries had signed the agreement. In 2017, France declared that they would ban gas- and diesel-powered cars by 2040. Norway said they would make this same ban, but by 2025. The Netherlands agreed to also ban these cars by 2030. However, in 2017, the United States withdrew from the Paris Agreement. However, there is hope that the United States will recommit to the Paris Agreement in the future.

Urban Heat Islands

A number of experts believe that one key to fighting heat waves is for people to avoid congregating in—or constructing—urban heat islands.

An urban heat island, or UHI, is an area that is hotter than surrounding areas due mainly to greater density of population and development. Typically, UHIs are made up of concentrated

This is an example of an urban heat island in New York City.

dwellings that house a great many people. These areas are sometimes 2°F to 20°F (1.1°C to 11.1°C) hotter due to high population. This is due to a lack of shade trees and an abundance of buildings and roofs made out of materials like asphalt, brick, stone, tar, and cement—all of which absorb, rather than reflect, the heat of the sun. Living within a UHI during a heat wave can be terribly dangerous. Stuart Gaffin, a research scientist with the Earth Institute at Columbia University, explains, "So we have two forces—urban heat islands and global warming—that are reinforcing each other and are going to create hot conditions for more than half the world's population."

Gaffin has conducted a great deal of research and analysis on how cities can help lower the heat emitted within UHIs. Some of the most effective measures include planting trees and creating rooftop gardens. By covering heat-absorbing rooftops with plants and other greenery, Gaffin and his research team

ARCHITECTURAL SOLUTIONS

An example of a LEED-certified building welcomes people inside.

One of the groups that is trying to make a difference in the planet's climate is the US Green Building Council (USGBC). Its stated mission is "to transform the way buildings and communities are designed, built, and operated, enabling an environmentally and socially responsible, healthy, and prosperous environment that improves the quality of life."

The USGBC sponsors the Leadership in Energy and Environmental Design (LEED) program, a voluntary national certification system that encourages architects and their clients to design and construct green and sustainable buildings. This program champions design methods that maximize energy efficiency, water-use reduction, the use of recycled materials, sustainable site development, and indoor environmental quality. The USGBC and the LEED program also educate architects, clients, builders, and the general public about the harm of urban heat islands and the design and construction strategies and materials that can be used to counteract them by incorporating cool, green spaces instead.

observed a huge difference in temperatures. In fact, rooftops covered in vegetation were more than 50°F (28°C) cooler than standard rooftops.

While creating rooftop gardens is effective, it can be expensive. Rooftop gardens can also require extra measures to be taken to protect the roof and support the extra weight of the dirt and plants. Even so, green rooftops might be one of people's best choices to beat the heat. "Can we air condition our way out of these heat waves? Not always," Gaffin says. "So how can we cool these cities down? There aren't many strategies we can choose. But green roofing looks like a great way to alleviate these problems."

Alternative Energy Sources

Clearly, one of the best ways to mitigate future heat waves is through decreasing the amount of greenhouse gases that go into the air, trapping heat and intensifying its buildup. That is, of course, much easier said than done, or it would have been done years ago. Reducing greenhouse gases means shifting the world away from the burning of fossil fuels for energy and transportation and toward the use of alternative energy sources like hydropower, wind power, solar power, and nuclear power.

Although these choices require immense technology, time, money, and corporate, governmental, and popular support to enact, many of these solutions are already being implemented. More than 3.6 million home solar panels have been installed in

PHOTOVOLTAIC SYSTEMS

Solar energy was first discovered in 1839 by Alexandre-Edmond Becquerel, who realized that sunlight could create an electric current. In 1883, Charles Fritts successfully generated electricity by coating a selenium plate with a thin layer of gold and putting it in the sunshine. This was a photovoltaic system. Fritts's invention has been refined by scientists since the late 1800s. Today, solar energy is an affordable way for people who live in more remote areas to get electricity. They don't have to be part of an electrical grid in order to get energy. In the floating islands of Lake Titicaca in South America, people are installing solar panels on their reed huts. This is an example of finding new, creative solutions to the problems of climate change.

Bangladesh. Solar panels are becoming more affordable, and countries and citizens are quickly adapting.

These are positive steps in the right direction, but change sometimes happens slowly. Even if we stopped all carbon emissions today, the climate would take a long time to fully adjust back to pre-industrial levels. Therefore, it's important to get as much information about disaster relief as possible.

Brenda Birkbeck evacuates her pets from the Californian Camp Fire in 2018.

CHAPTER 4

Stay Informed

Knowledge is an important aspect of fighting climate change. The more we know, the more damage we can prevent. Although we are trying to decrease global temperatures and find solutions to energy problems, knowledge is still important if you do find yourself in a heat wave or forest fire.

Ten Tips

What can you do to help yourself and your friends, family, and neighbors cope when a heat wave or forest fire occurs in your community? It may seem like a number of the most important steps are completely out of your hands and under the control of government committees and national organizations. However, here are ten simple steps you can take to help keep you and the people you care about safe before and during a heat wave:

1. Listen to local weather warnings. Turn to the weather report and check for forecast updates. If the prediction includes a heat wave or forest fire, don't wait to see if it will happen. Assume that it will, and prepare right away.

2. Make sure there is enough fluid in the house for everyone. Dehydration is one of the most serious consequences of a heat wave and is dangerous for everyone, but especially for the very young or old. It is important to have enough water and clear juices in the house so that everyone stays hydrated. Soft drinks, coffee, alcohol, and any sugary and/or caffeinated drinks do not hydrate the body and should be avoided.

3. If asked to evacuate in the middle of a forest fire, then really evacuate. Although it may be hard to leave your home behind, it is much better to lose physical items than your life.

4. Wear proper clothing during a heat wave. It should be loose, made out of a light, breathable material, and be white or light in color so that it doesn't absorb heat. If you live in an extremely high-risk area, you might want to invest in special clothing designed to keep the body cool.

5. Limit physical activity. This is not the time for a bike ride or quick game of basketball in the backyard. Stay inside and out of the sun, and try to do any necessary outside work in the cooler, early morning hours.

6. Go outside cautiously. If you do go outside, make sure to apply sunscreen and stay in the shade as much as possible. Wear a wide-brimmed hat for additional shade.

7. Never leave a child or pet inside a car in the summer heat. It is surprising how fast the inside of a car can heat up. A dark dashboard or upholstery can quickly reach temperatures of 180°F to 200°F (82°C to 93°C). Experts have shown that if it is 80°F (27°C) outside, within an hour it can be more than 120°F (49°C) inside a vehicle. On a 95°F (35°C) day, a car can reach 150°F (66°C) in less than an hour. Never leave a child or a pet alone in a car because it will become dangerously hot in mere minutes. Every year, there are scores of horrific news reports concerning deaths of small children and pets in sealed and parked cars. Nearly every time, the parent or pet owner says he or she was away from the car for "just a few minutes."

8. Keep an updated list of places to go within your community to get cool. These can include libraries, schools, community pools, malls, theaters, and recreational centers. Know what days and hours they are open.

9. Help combat global warming. Simple ways to help fight against global warming are to take steps at home such as recycling, carpooling, biking, composting organic food waste, and conserving water.

10. Don't give up hope. Large policy changes and small changes in lifestyle can make a big difference. Remember that if we work together and treat climate

change as something that we can fix, we may be able to create positive outcomes.

FEMA Heat Wave Recommendations

The Federal Emergency Management Agency (FEMA) has a number of recommendations for anyone who is exposed to a heat wave. Once a warning has been issued, you should:

1. Install air conditioners if possible and check ducts for proper insulation.
2. Put aluminum-covered cardboard in between windows and drapes to reflect the sun and heat back outside.
3. Cover windows that receive morning or afternoon sun with drapes, shades, or outdoor awnings.

If you don't have air conditioning, install fans in each room. Ceiling fans are ideal, but portable box fans can also help. Preparation is a key to survival. Understanding how at risk your community is for a heat wave and then taking precautions if you find yourself in a heat wave may help avoid heat-related illness.

Illnesses from Heat

Heat can affect the human body in many different ways. Health conditions that result from overheating include heat rash, heat cramps, heat exhaustion or fatigue, heat syncope, and

Problem	Symptoms	Treatment
heat rash	irritated skin due to excessive sweating; red cluster of small blisters, usually found on neck, upper chest, groin, and creases of elbow	Keep affected area dry; apply dusting powder.
heat cramps	heavy sweating, painful cramps in muscles of legs and/or abdomen due to low salt levels from perspiration	Stop moving and sit still, drink water or clear juice, and seek help if spasms don't subside within an hour.
heat exhaustion/ fatigue	heavy sweating, extreme weakness, dizziness, confusion, nausea, muscle cramps, elevated body temperature, fast and shallow breathing	Rest in a cool area, drink plenty of water, and take a cool shower or bath.
heat syncope	fainting or dizziness, often following rising from a sitting position	Sit or lie down in a cool place; drink water or clear juice.
heatstroke (also known as sunstroke)	hot and dry skin, profuse sweating, hallucinations, chills, throbbing headache, high body temperature, confusion, dizziness, slurred speech	Call 911 (this is a potentially fatal condition), move to a shaded area, soak clothes with water, and fan the body.

heatstroke. Knowing the difference between them and how each one is treated is vital. Be on the lookout for symptoms in yourself and those around you, and seek medical attention at the first sign of them.

It is important to be informed in case of emergency. Knowing the signs and symptoms of heat-related illness is essential for your

HEAT WAVE CLASSIFICATIONS

The National Weather Service issues warnings to the public about excessive and dangerous heat, just as it does for other types of severe weather, such as tornadoes and hurricanes.

EXCESSIVE HEAT OUTLOOK: This warning is issued when the potential for excessive heat exists within the next three to seven days.

EXCESSIVE HEAT WATCH: This warning is issued to the public when a heat event will occur in the next twenty-four to seventy-two hours.

EXCESSIVE HEAT ADVISORY: This warning is issued when dangerously hot conditions will occur within twelve hours.

EXCESSIVE HEAT WARNING: This warning is issued when the heat, or a combination of heat and humidity, will be intense enough to inconvenience most of the population.

How do the experts know when to issue a particular warning? They base it largely on the heat index. If the heat index (relative humidity added to actual air temperature) is expected to exceed 105°F (41°C) for at least two consecutive days, an excessive heat warning is issued. The heat index is not a measure of actual temperature, but a measure of how hot it feels when you step outside (working in much the same way as the wind chill index does during the winter months). Humidity makes already high temperatures feel even hotter and more oppressive.

The heat index also details possible negative health consequences of various levels of heat:

80°F to 90°F (27°C to 32°C)	possible fatigue with prolonged physical activity
90°F to 105°F (32°C to 41°C)	possible sunstroke, heat cramps, and heat exhaustion with prolonged physical activity
105°F to 130°F (41°C to 54°C)	greater chance of sunstroke, heat cramps, and heat exhaustion with prolonged activity
130°F and higher (54°C and higher)	sunstroke, heat cramps, and heat exhaustion likely with prolonged physical activity

and others' survival. Consider taking an emergency-response class with the Red Cross so that you will be trained in case you find yourself in an emergency situation. Remember that unpredictable weather patterns are now a common part of our daily lives, and we need to know what to do in case we find ourselves in an emergency.

Greta Thunberg strikes for the climate in Hamburg, Germany, in 2019.

CHAPTER 5

Young Activists

In addition to helping community members when a heat wave does strike, consider changing policy. There are many young activists who are standing up to policy-makers, companies, and their own schools in order to demand more responsible action.

Greta Thunberg

Take Greta Thunberg, for instance. She is a teenage activist from Sweden. In August 2018, she started to boycott her school in order to promote better climate decision-making. She has started a revolution called "School Strike 4 Climate Action." Students around the world have been joining Thunberg's cause. More than twenty thousand students have held strikes in nearly three hundred cities around the world.

Thunberg has given a TED talk and has spoken at the UN Climate Change COP24 Conference. She urges policy-makers, companies, and citizens to stop emitting carbon into the atmosphere. She places focus on the environment, rather than money, questioning our large-scale emphasis on profit over preservation. She believes that children must change the world since adults are not talking about climate change nearly enough to create wide-scale change. Thunberg imagines her own future as dire and worries for the lives of her future children and grandchildren. By protesting, she is calling worldwide attention to climate change and demanding that policy-makers listen to her. Just like Julia Butterfly Hill, Greta Thunberg is an activist who is speaking out. Both of these people show that you are never too young or too small to make a large and lasting difference.

Get Involved!

You can also change the world. The damage from any natural disaster can be reduced if enough people in the community volunteer to help. What can you do to help your friends and neighbors? Get involved! Here are some suggestions to get started:

1. Join a national environmental organization, and then attend local chapter meetings or start your own. Check with your guidance counselor at school for possible resources, or go online and contact groups like the Environmental Defense Fund or Power Shift Network.

2. At school, volunteer to teach or lead a workshop designed to inform students about the threats involved and how individuals can best respond to them.

3. Put together a number of emergency supply packs and distribute them at local community centers or other organizations that would appreciate them.

4. Join disaster organizations like the Red Cross and find out what you can do to help.

5. Carry a reusable water bottle around wherever you go.

6. Put out bowls of water for pets and wildlife to use.

7. Write about climate change for your school newspaper.

8. Sponsor a Help Your Neighbor program to keep an eye on people who live alone, are ill, or are elderly. You can take charge of calling these people once a day to make sure they are handling the heat. You can also go with your parents or other adults to visit these people. Upon arrival, make sure they have the supplies that they need, check that their air conditioners are working properly, and transport them to cooling spots throughout the city if necessary.

Community Support

Communities come together in the aftermath of all sorts of disasters. After wildfires broke out in Slapout, Oklahoma, in 2017, people from all over the nation sent supplies and money. Unsolicited donations appeared in the Great Plains. Ranchers and farmers received money, water, formula for newborn calves, food for cattle, winter clothes, and even cheese from Wisconsin. These

UNEXPECTED OUTCOMES

Changing temperatures certainly keep everyone on their toes, especially anthropologists. In 2018, a surprising thing happened as a result of a heat wave in the fields of England: high temperatures allowed anthropologists to see ancient structural remains. The temperature changed the consistency of the soil, and aerial photographs revealed stunning historic sites, dating back to the Neolithic and Iron Ages. Researchers were also able to see the remains of Roman farms and several burial and ceremonial sites. This unusual consequence only proves how willing to adapt humans must be.

donations did not come from the government but from people around the country who knew these people were suffering. That demonstrates the power of community.

Igniting the Planet

Overall, heat waves and forest fires are a problem no matter when or where they happen. Heat waves hover over a region, refusing to budge and making it hard for everyone to get through each day. Forest fires threaten people's health—physical and mental—and they tax local infrastructure in many unseen ways. Heat waves cannot currently be stopped. Instead, humans must learn how to reduce the risk as much as possible by facing the challenges of global warming, even as we learn how to handle soaring temperatures when they arrive.

A study published in *Nature Communications* in January of 2019 found that heat waves hit developing nations more severely than developed countries. As the population increases, heat waves will become a major concern for countries in Asia, like India. In the second half of the 21st century, these countries will likely be hit the hardest by heat waves.

However, it's wrong to say that heat waves don't pose a risk for more developed countries. In 2013, Dr. Robin Ikeda, an administrator at the National Center for Environmental Health and Agency for Toxic Substances and Disease Registry, stated, "No one should die from a heat wave, but every year on average, extreme heat causes 658 deaths in the United States—more than tornadoes, hurricanes, floods, and lightning combined."

Although there are many solutions, many motivated people, and much activism going on, changing an entire planet's climate is slow work. However, this does not mean that we shouldn't strive for change. When Julia Butterfly Hill sat in her tree, she wasn't sure if she could convince the lumber mill to not cut the tree down, but she sat there anyway—day after day. There are people all around us who are committed to making small changes. When we work together as a global community, we can ignite the planet, not with fire or heat, but with ideas—new and fresh ones that can transform the world.

Glossary

acclimatize To adapt or become accustomed to a new climate or environment.

Anthropocene The age of humans.

carbon dioxide A greenhouse gas naturally present in the air but also produced by the burning of fossil fuels.

climate Atmospheric changes in a region over a long period of time.

climate change A long-term change in Earth's climate, which today is seen as a result of human activity.

conifer An evergreen tree.

dehydration An abnormal loss of water from the body, typically due to perspiration.

ecosystem A community of organisms functioning as one unit.

emission Something that is produced and sent or released into the open.

evacuate To leave a place of danger and go to a safe place.

fossil fuel A fuel, such as coal, oil, or natural gas, formed by the decomposition of prehistoric organisms.

global warming A significant and sustained increase in global surface and ocean temperatures; a consequence of human activity (such as the burning of fossil fuels) and the buildup of heat-trapping carbon emissions and other greenhouse gases in the atmosphere.

greenhouse effect The trapping of the sun's warmth in Earth's lower atmosphere.

greenhouse gas A gas, such as carbon dioxide or methane, that contributes to the greenhouse effect in our atmosphere.

Holocene The current period of time in Earth's history.

infrastructure Buildings, bridges, tunnels, railways, roads, sewers, electrical grids, telecommunications, and other physical and organizational structures needed for the operation of a society.

megafire A fire that burns more than 100,000 acres (40,470 hectares).

mitigate To make less serious, severe, or painful; to lessen the gravity of a situation.

photovoltaic The production of electricity when two substances are joined and exposed to light.

vegetation Plants considered collectively, especially those in a specific ecosystem or habitat.

Further Information

Books

Bjornerud, Marcia. *Timefulness: How Thinking Like a Geologist Can Help Save the World*. Princeton, NJ: Princeton University Press, 2018.

Climate Refugees: How Climate Change Is Displacing Millions. New York, NY: New York Times Educational Publishing in Association with The Rosen Publishing Group, 2019.

Emanuel, Kerry. *What We Know About Climate Change*. Cambridge, MA: MIT Press, 2012.

Jackson, M. *The Secret Lives of Glaciers*. Brattleboro, VT: Green Writers Press, 2019.

Shea, Therese. *Droughts and Heat Waves*. New York, NY: PowerKids Press, 2019.

Vollmann, William T. *No Immediate Danger: Volume One of Carbon Ideologies*. New York, NY: Penguin Publishing Group, 2018.

Websites

NASA: Global Climate Change
https://climate.nasa.gov/evidence/
This is a site about global warming that includes charts and graphs.

National Geographic: **What Is Global Warming, Explained**
https://www.nationalgeographic.com/environment/
global-warming/global-warming-overview
This site explains the causes and effects of global warming.

United Nations Climate Change Conferences
https://unfccc.int/process/conferences/what-are-
united-nations-climate-change-conferences
This site details how the United Nations holds conferences to address climate change.

Organizations

CAMEL Climate Change Education,
Science Education Resource Center at Carleton College
One North College Street
Northfield, MN 55057
(507) 222-4368
Website: https://camelclimatechange.org/138312
CAMEL is a multimedia resource for educators funded by
the National Science Foundation. It promotes mitigation and
adaptation strategies relating to climate change.

Friends of the Earth
1101 15th Street NW, 11th Floor
Washington, DC 20005
(202) 783-7400
Website: http://www.foe.org
Working with a network of grassroots groups in seventy-
seven countries, Friends of the Earth defends the environment
and champions a more healthy and just world. Its current
campaigns focus on clean energy and solutions to global
warming; protecting people from toxic and new, potentially
harmful technologies; and promoting smarter, low-pollution
transportation alternatives.

Union of Concerned Scientists
Two Brattle Sq.
Cambridge, MA 02138-3780
(617) 547-5552
Website: https://www.ucsusa.org
The Union of Concerned Scientists is a group of 250 scientists
who use advocacy and scientific research to create solutions
for climate change.

Selected Bibliography

Congressional Budget Office. *Potential Impacts of Climate Change in the United States.* Washington, DC: Congressional Budget Office, 2009.

Cullen, Heidi. *The Weather of the Future: Heat Waves, Extreme Storms, and Other Scenes from a Climate-Changed Planet.* New York, NY: Harper, 2010.

Delano, Marfe Ferguson. *Earth in the Hot Seat: Bulletins from a Warming World.* Des Moines, IA: National Geographic Children's Books, 2009.

Eckholm, Erik. "Heat ... Wave? Bubble? Dome? Seeking an Apt Name as the Hot Days Pile Up." *New York Times*, July 22, 2011. http://www.nytimes.com/2011/07/23/us/23dome.html.

Frazier, Ian. "The Day the Great Plains Burned." *New Yorker*, November 5, 2018. https://www.newyorker.com/magazine/2018/11/05/the-day-the-great-plains-burned.

Garthwaite, Josie. "Stanford Study Shows Regions Increasingly Suffer Hot, Dry Conditions at the Same Time." *Stanford News*, November 28, 2018. https://news.stanford.edu/2018/11/28/hot-dry-years-will-hit-many-regions-simultaneously.

Hannam, Peter. "Why Aren't They Doing Anything?: Students Strike to Give Climate Lesson." *Sydney Morning Herald*, November 25, 2018. https://www.smh.com.au/environment/climate-change/why-aren-t-they-doing-anything-students-strike-to-give-climate-lesson-20181123-p50hvu.html.

Katcher, Marcie. "NOAA Heat/Health Watch Warning System Improving Forecasts and Warnings for Excessive Heat." NOAA, January 11, 2005. http://www.noaanews.noaa.gov/stories2005/s2366.htm.

King, Ledyard. "Climate Change: Meet the Florida Congresswoman Leading the House Charge." *USA Today*, January 11, 2019. https://www.usatoday.com/story/news/politics/2019/01/10/climate-change-chair-new-house-panel-presses-dramatic-response/2465450002.

Lallanilla, Marc. "The Life of Tree-Sitter Julia Hill." *Spruce*, updated January 30, 2019. https://www.thespruce.com/the-life-of-julia-hill-1708797.

Murphy, Anthony. "Heatwave Reveals England's Lost Prehistoric Sites." BBC News, August 15, 2018. https://www.bbc.com/news/uk-england-45170581.

Ocko, Ilissa, and Monika Barcikowska. "How Can Half a Degree of Warming Matter So Much?" Environmental Defense Fund, October 18, 2018. https://www.edf.org/blog/2018/10/18/how-can-half-degree-warming-matter-so-much.

Patterson, Thom. "Heat Pops Pipes Nationwide; Brace for Higher Bills." CNN, August 14, 2011. http://www.cnn.com/2011/US/08/13/water.infrastructure/index.html.

Quackenbush, Casey. "A Record-Breaking Heatwave Is Scorching Australia." *Time*, January 18, 2019. http://time.com/5506684/australia-record-breaking-heatwave-2019.

Rice, Doyle, and Luke Kerr-Dineen. "Outreach Efforts Help Save Lives in Heat Wave." *USA Today*, July 21, 2011. http://www.usatoday.com/weather/news/extremes/2011-07-20-heat-wave-record-temperatures_n.htm.

Schneider, Bonnie. *Extreme Weather*. New York, NY: Palgrave Macmillan, 2012.

Stromberg, Joseph. "What Is the Anthropocene and Are We in It?" *Smithsonian*, January 2013. https://www.smithsonianmag.com/science-nature/what-is-the-anthropocene-and-are-we-in-it-164801414.

Index

Page numbers in **boldface** refer to images.

About The Author

Alex David has her MFA from New England State College. She has written a series of books called *We the Weirdos*. Her poems and short stories have been published in literary journals such as *Green Mountains Review* and *Adelaide Literary Magazine*. Additionally, she has taught a class on eco-fiction at Canisius College in Buffalo, New York. She loves to learn and write about climate science. She is hopeful for the future.